Nathan's New School

By Jordan Lane

Illustrated by Jeremy Tugeau

Nathan's mouth was dry. He was sure the butterflies in his stomach were having a party. He tripped over the sidewalk trying to keep up with his sister, Alexis.

"Don't stumble!" Alexis growled. Nathan couldn't help it—he was so nervous about his first day at Bright Mountain Middle School. He was counting down the days until the weekend.

"Why are you so nervous?" asked Alexis. Nathan scowled. The reason was obvious: he was the new kid!

"Nobody asked me if I wanted to move," he grumbled. "Guess what, I didn't."

Nathan missed everything about South Carolina—the mouse family that lived in their old farmhouse, the sounds of the owls at nighttime, and the summer rainstorms. More importantly, he missed his friends, especially Myles, his best friend since kindergarten.

Nathan whispered under his breath, "My worst nightmare has come true!"

When they reached the bus stop Alexis said, "Give the school a try—you might like it!" Then she pushed Nathan onto the bus.

He slid into an empty seat near the back of the bus and stared out the window.

When the bus arrived at school, Nathan sighed and hoped he wouldn't get sick. He saw a bunch of kids racing up the marble steps.

Oh, good, we've arrived, Nathan thought.

Bright Mountain Middle School was the complete opposite of Nathan's old school. The hallways were crowded and loud. Nathan was convinced that there must be a thousand kids and they all knew each other. He was sure that everyone was glaring at him as he wandered through the hallway with his burning red face.

I'll probably find my homeroom next week, he thought. He was surprised how easily he found the classroom! "I have to memorize this route," he told himself.

Nathan never had time for artistic endeavors in the country, but now he would. His next class was art. He wasn't exactly sure what you did in art class. *This could be weird,* he thought.

It turned out art class was pretty cool. With nimble fingers, he dabbled the paint to create the sunny, tropical picture of a Carolina seacoast. His teacher said it was a "sensational creation!" Nathan never knew he had artistic abilities.

The bell rang and Nathan struggled through the hallway to his next class: science!

Science had never been his favorite subject in South Carolina. He hoped it would be better here. The teacher was an older man who was also the basketball coach.

"Welcome, Nathan," Mr. Erickson said. "I hope you like our school. If you like, let's call your mom later and ask if you can come to basketball practice today. I will introduce you to the other students."

Before long, it was lunchtime. Nathan's lab partner, Tony, asked him to sit at the table with a bunch of his buddies. Tony introduced Nathan to the other boys.

"Finish your lunch quickly; let's play basketball," Tony shouted to Nathan. "We desperately need a point guard."

Nathan raced to the court. "This school isn't awful. I can't believe Alexis was whining about going to a new school," Nathan laughed as he made the game-winning free throw.